When Rusty Went Driving

by Connie Dunn

When Rusty Went Driving ©2013 Connie Dunn

Published by Nature Woman Wisdom Press

First Edition. Printed and bound in the United States of America.

All rights reserved. No part of this book may be reproduced in any form or by any electronic or mechanical means, including information storage and retrieval systems, recording, or photocopying, without permission in writing from the publisher, except by a reviewer, who may quote brief passages in review or where permitted by law.

Copyright ©2013 Connie Dunn
ISBN-13: 978-0615931067
ISBN-10: 0615931065

Published by Nature Woman Wisdom Press

Printed in The United States of America

Library of Congress Cataloging in Publication Data
Dunn, Connie
  When Rusty Went Driving
Children
  When Rusty Went Driving
  by Connie Dunn
Dogs
  When Rusty Went Driving
  by Connie Dunn
Chihuahuas
  When Rusty Went Driving
  by Connie Dunn

ACKNOWLEGEMENTS

Photos by:

Joyce Adams,

Connie Dunn, and

Linda Elsmore

"Even the tiniest Poodle or Chihuahua is still a wolf at heart." - Dorothy Hinshaw Patent, Dogs: The Wolf Within

"My little dog---a heartbeat at my feet." - Edith Wharton

for Rusty Toolittle
(subject of book and Chihuahua featured in photos)

my wife, Joyce

my friend, Linda

for all Chihuahua lovers everywhere

"The average dog is a nicer person than the average person." - Andrew A. Rooney

"Dogs never bite me. Just humans."
— Marilyn Monroe

WHEN RUSTY WENT DRIVING

It was a beautiful day in New England, the day Rusty decided to drive. He loved driving just about anywhere.

"Come on everybody!" Rusty squeaked.

Rusty rarely barked. It was a long time before he ever made a sound, so Rusty's family was somewhat worried. Rusty was a "rescue" dog. Someone had left him outside the doors of the Veterinarian's Office.

The vet examined him. He was very small and had some bad teeth. Once the vet removed his infected teeth, the technicians eagerly fed him warmed dog food.

He went to live with his new family, who learned that Rusty's squeaking was definitely his way of communicating.

And when Rusty wanted to drive…

Well, they were accommodating!

Who could resist this face! So off they went to see New England's beautiful sites!

Rusty didn't like the ocean, unless he saw it from his mommy's pouch!

"I'll just ride, okay?"

"Okay!" says Momma.

We went to this creek to walk in the fall and…

Again in the Winter!

Rusty didn't mind walking on the pavement.

But walking in the snow was just no place for a tiny Chihuahua.

"Sometimes the best place to be is curled up with a warm blanket in my chair," says Rusty. "Especially when Mom wants to see the ocean in the middle of the winter."

"Momma always says that it's too long to wait to see the Ocean from summer to summer…so we always have to drive to the Ocean in the winter. The bright side of that…I get to drive!"

"Brrrrrrrr!" says Rusty.

"Is this really important, Momma?" Rusty asks.

Even though the snowfalls can be deep, there's always the hope of Spring.

I like to sun myself!" says Rusty. "And a good walk in the sunny woods is okay, too. It can't stay winter forever!"

"The smell of green leaves is beautiful!" says Rusty.

"Hey, are there any Bears or Moose in here?" he asks.

Here's Moose Rusty! He doesn't appear to think it's as funny as Momma and her friends do!

Mommas do interesting things to their Chihuahuas, this is true! Of course, that does include carrying them in their pouches.

"But then, from time to time, I do look like a Momma Kangaroo with my little Roo on board!" says Momma.

"We look good!" says Rusty. "I just need my big hat, too!"

"You mean your Sombrero?" asks Momma.

"Yeah! You gotta problem with that?" asks Rusty.

"No, I just thought you didn't like hats!" Momma answers.

"It depends," he says confidently.

"Well, it's getting cold again, can we go driving? The leaves should be falling!"

"Oh my little man," says Momma. "We can go driving and see the beautiful New England countryside in all its beautiful colors. Let's get your other mother and Auntie Linda!"

"I'm ready! Is everyone seat-belted in? It could be a bumpy ride!"

So everyone got into the car, and off they went in search of New England's beautiful scenery with cameras in hand!

"Is there anything as beautiful as a waterfall?" Rusty wonders.

Momma says, "The Heron in front of the waterfall!"

"Oh," said Rusty. "I didn't see it!"

"Rusty," says Momma, "That's why you have to sit and watch the landscape for a while. It's only when you pay attention that you can see all the details."

"Details?" asks Rusty. "I just want to drive!"

"You'll get to drive soon!" Momma assures.

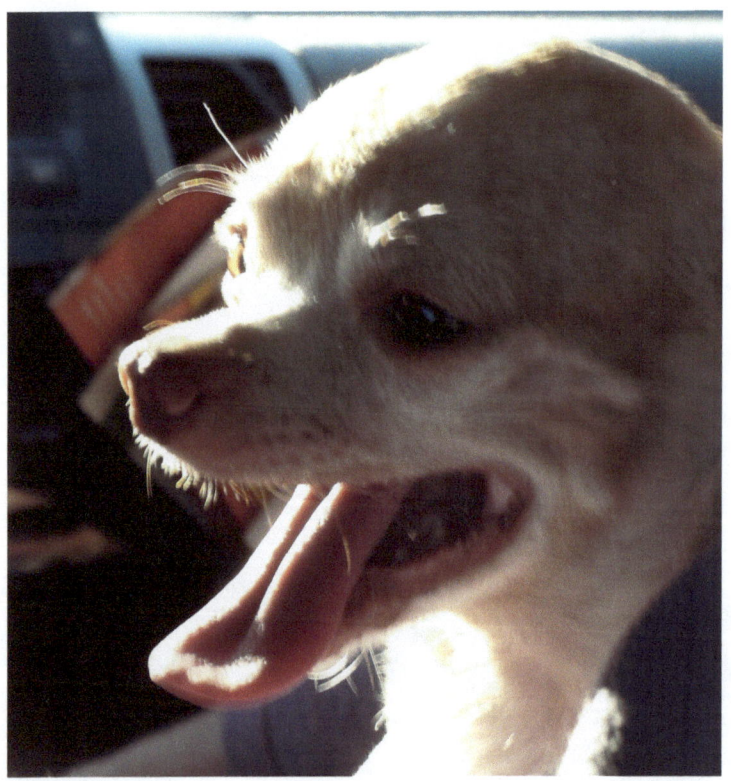

"Oh, Goodie! Everyone get in! It's time to go...it's time to go!"

"Okay, okay! I'm in," says Auntie Linda.

Momma J says, "Okay, I'm ready, Rusty."

"Let's go! Let's go! Let's go!" Rusty pants.

"Settle down, Rusty," Momma says. "We'll be home soon."

Momma J says, "Yes, Sophie will be waiting for us all!"

"Oh, so you brought the d-o-g home! I was hoping you'd lose him," says Sophie.

"Not a chance, butterball!" says Rusty. "I always come home!"

The End

www.ingramcontent.com/pod-product-compliance
Lightning Source LLC
Chambersburg PA
CBHW041810040426
42449CB00001B/43